50 United Kingdom Pizza Recipes for Home

By: Kelly Johnson

Table of Contents

- Margherita Pizza
- Pepperoni Pizza
- Hawaiian Pizza
- BBQ Chicken Pizza
- Vegetable Supreme Pizza
- Meat Feast Pizza
- Four Cheese Pizza
- Mushroom and Spinach Pizza
- Spicy Sausage Pizza
- Pesto Chicken Pizza
- Mediterranean Pizza
- Smoked Salmon Pizza
- Roasted Garlic and Chicken Pizza
- Sweetcorn and Bacon Pizza
- Artichoke and Olive Pizza
- Tandoori Chicken Pizza
- Spinach and Feta Pizza
- Caprese Pizza
- Meatball Pizza
- Buffalo Chicken Pizza
- Prosciutto and Arugula Pizza
- Goat Cheese and Caramelized Onion Pizza
- Fig and Gorgonzola Pizza
- Shrimp Scampi Pizza
- Chicken Alfredo Pizza
- Steak and Blue Cheese Pizza
- Sundried Tomato and Pesto Pizza
- Roasted Vegetable Pizza
- White Clam Pizza
- Thai Chicken Pizza
- Brie and Cranberry Pizza
- Pulled Pork Pizza
- Barbecue Bacon Pizza
- Sausage and Ricotta Pizza
- Chicken Tikka Masala Pizza

- Philly Cheesesteak Pizza
- Margherita with Balsamic Glaze Pizza
- Teriyaki Chicken Pizza
- Greek Pizza
- Asparagus and Goat Cheese Pizza
- Cajun Shrimp Pizza
- Fennel and Sausage Pizza
- Truffle Mushroom Pizza
- Pear and Gorgonzola Pizza
- Peking Duck Pizza
- Ratatouille Pizza
- Reuben Pizza
- Crab and Avocado Pizza
- Fig and Prosciutto Pizza
- Breakfast Pizza

Margherita Pizza

Ingredients:

- 1 pizza dough (store-bought or homemade)
- 1 cup pizza sauce
- 2 cups shredded mozzarella cheese
- 2-3 ripe tomatoes, thinly sliced
- Fresh basil leaves
- Olive oil
- Salt and pepper to taste

Instructions:

Preheat your oven to 475°F (245°C). If using a pizza stone, place it in the oven to preheat as well.
Roll out the pizza dough on a floured surface to your desired thickness. Transfer it to a pizza peel or a lightly greased baking sheet.
Spread the pizza sauce evenly over the dough, leaving a small border around the edges.
Sprinkle the shredded mozzarella cheese over the sauce.
Arrange the thinly sliced tomatoes on top of the cheese.
Drizzle a little olive oil over the tomatoes and season with salt and pepper to taste.
Carefully transfer the pizza to the preheated oven or pizza stone.
Bake for 10-12 minutes, or until the crust is golden brown and the cheese is bubbly and melted.
Remove the pizza from the oven and let it cool slightly.
Garnish with fresh basil leaves before serving. Slice and enjoy your delicious Margherita pizza!

Pepperoni Pizza

Ingredients:

- 1 pizza dough (store-bought or homemade)
- 1 cup pizza sauce
- 2 cups shredded mozzarella cheese
- 30-40 slices pepperoni
- Olive oil
- Dried oregano
- Crushed red pepper flakes (optional)

- Grated Parmesan cheese (optional)

Instructions:

Preheat your oven to 475°F (245°C). If using a pizza stone, place it in the oven to preheat as well.

Roll out the pizza dough on a floured surface to your desired thickness. Transfer it to a pizza peel or a lightly greased baking sheet.

Spread the pizza sauce evenly over the dough, leaving a small border around the edges.

Sprinkle the shredded mozzarella cheese over the sauce.

Arrange the pepperoni slices on top of the cheese.

Drizzle a little olive oil over the pepperoni.

Sprinkle dried oregano and crushed red pepper flakes (if using) over the pizza for added flavor.

Carefully transfer the pizza to the preheated oven or pizza stone.

Bake for 10-12 minutes, or until the crust is golden brown and the cheese is bubbly and melted.

Remove the pizza from the oven and let it cool slightly.

Optionally, sprinkle grated Parmesan cheese over the hot pizza before serving.

Slice and enjoy your delicious pepperoni pizza!

Hawaiian Pizza

Ingredients:

- 1 pizza dough (store-bought or homemade)
- 1/2 cup pizza sauce
- 2 cups shredded mozzarella cheese
- 1 cup diced ham or Canadian bacon
- 1 cup pineapple chunks (fresh or canned)
- Olive oil
- Salt and pepper to taste

Instructions:

Preheat your oven to 475°F (245°C). If using a pizza stone, place it in the oven to preheat as well.

Roll out the pizza dough on a floured surface to your desired thickness. Transfer it to a pizza peel or a lightly greased baking sheet.

Spread the pizza sauce evenly over the dough, leaving a small border around the edges.

Sprinkle the shredded mozzarella cheese over the sauce.

Evenly distribute the diced ham or Canadian bacon and pineapple chunks over the cheese.

Drizzle a little olive oil over the toppings and season with salt and pepper to taste.

Carefully transfer the pizza to the preheated oven or pizza stone.

Bake for 10-12 minutes, or until the crust is golden brown and the cheese is bubbly and melted.

Remove the pizza from the oven and let it cool slightly.

Slice and enjoy your delicious Hawaiian pizza!

BBQ Chicken Pizza

Ingredients:

- 1 pizza dough (store-bought or homemade)
- 1/2 cup barbecue sauce
- 2 cups cooked chicken breast, shredded or diced
- 1 cup shredded mozzarella cheese
- 1/2 cup red onion, thinly sliced
- 1/4 cup fresh cilantro, chopped
- Olive oil
- Salt and pepper to taste

Instructions:

Preheat your oven to 475°F (245°C). If using a pizza stone, place it in the oven to preheat as well.

Roll out the pizza dough on a floured surface to your desired thickness. Transfer it to a pizza peel or a lightly greased baking sheet.

Spread the barbecue sauce evenly over the dough, leaving a small border around the edges.

Sprinkle the shredded mozzarella cheese over the barbecue sauce.

Distribute the cooked chicken breast evenly over the cheese.

Scatter the thinly sliced red onion over the chicken.

Drizzle a little olive oil over the toppings and season with salt and pepper to taste.

Carefully transfer the pizza to the preheated oven or pizza stone.

Bake for 10-12 minutes, or until the crust is golden brown and the cheese is bubbly and melted.

Remove the pizza from the oven and sprinkle chopped fresh cilantro over the top.

Let the pizza cool slightly before slicing and serving. Enjoy your delicious BBQ chicken pizza!

Vegetable Supreme Pizza

Ingredients:

- 1 pizza dough (store-bought or homemade)
- 1/2 cup pizza sauce
- 2 cups shredded mozzarella cheese
- 1 bell pepper, thinly sliced
- 1 small red onion, thinly sliced
- 1 small zucchini, thinly sliced
- 1 cup sliced mushrooms
- 1/2 cup sliced black olives
- 1/4 cup sliced cherry tomatoes
- 2 tablespoons olive oil
- 1 teaspoon dried oregano
- Salt and pepper to taste

Instructions:

Preheat your oven to 475°F (245°C). If using a pizza stone, place it in the oven to preheat as well.

Roll out the pizza dough on a floured surface to your desired thickness. Transfer it to a pizza peel or a lightly greased baking sheet.

Spread the pizza sauce evenly over the dough, leaving a small border around the edges.

Sprinkle the shredded mozzarella cheese over the sauce.

Arrange the thinly sliced bell pepper, red onion, zucchini, mushrooms, black olives, and cherry tomatoes over the cheese.

Drizzle olive oil over the vegetables and sprinkle with dried oregano. Season with salt and pepper to taste.

Carefully transfer the pizza to the preheated oven or pizza stone.

Bake for 10-12 minutes, or until the crust is golden brown and the cheese is bubbly and melted.

Remove the pizza from the oven and let it cool slightly.

Slice and serve your delicious vegetable supreme pizza! Enjoy the burst of flavors from the fresh veggies.

Meat Feast Pizza

Ingredients:

- 1 pizza dough (store-bought or homemade)
- 1/2 cup pizza sauce
- 2 cups shredded mozzarella cheese
- 1/2 cup cooked and crumbled Italian sausage
- 1/2 cup cooked and crumbled bacon
- 1/2 cup sliced pepperoni
- 1/2 cup sliced ham or Canadian bacon
- 1/4 cup sliced black olives (optional)
- 1/4 cup sliced red onions (optional)
- 1/4 cup sliced bell peppers (optional)
- 2 tablespoons olive oil
- 1 teaspoon dried oregano
- Salt and pepper to taste

Instructions:

Preheat your oven to 475°F (245°C). If using a pizza stone, place it in the oven to preheat as well.

Roll out the pizza dough on a floured surface to your desired thickness. Transfer it to a pizza peel or a lightly greased baking sheet.

Spread the pizza sauce evenly over the dough, leaving a small border around the edges.

Sprinkle the shredded mozzarella cheese over the sauce.

Evenly distribute the cooked and crumbled Italian sausage, bacon, pepperoni, and ham or Canadian bacon over the cheese.

If using, scatter the sliced black olives, red onions, and bell peppers over the toppings.

Drizzle olive oil over the toppings and sprinkle with dried oregano. Season with salt and pepper to taste.

Carefully transfer the pizza to the preheated oven or pizza stone.

Bake for 10-12 minutes, or until the crust is golden brown and the cheese is bubbly and melted.

Remove the pizza from the oven and let it cool slightly.

Slice and serve your delicious meat feast pizza! Enjoy the hearty combination of meats and flavors.

Four Cheese Pizza

Ingredients:

- 1 pizza dough (store-bought or homemade)
- 1/2 cup pizza sauce
- 1 cup shredded mozzarella cheese
- 1 cup shredded cheddar cheese
- 1/2 cup crumbled feta cheese
- 1/2 cup grated Parmesan cheese
- 2 tablespoons olive oil
- 2 cloves garlic, minced (optional)
- Fresh basil leaves for garnish (optional)
- Salt and pepper to taste

Instructions:

Preheat your oven to 475°F (245°C). If using a pizza stone, place it in the oven to preheat as well.
Roll out the pizza dough on a floured surface to your desired thickness. Transfer it to a pizza peel or a lightly greased baking sheet.
In a small bowl, mix together the olive oil and minced garlic, if using.
Brush the garlic-infused olive oil evenly over the surface of the pizza dough.
Spread the pizza sauce evenly over the dough, leaving a small border around the edges.
Sprinkle the shredded mozzarella cheese over the sauce.
Evenly distribute the shredded cheddar cheese, crumbled feta cheese, and grated Parmesan cheese over the pizza.
Season with salt and pepper to taste.
Carefully transfer the pizza to the preheated oven or pizza stone.
Bake for 10-12 minutes, or until the crust is golden brown and the cheese is bubbly and melted.
Remove the pizza from the oven and let it cool slightly.
Garnish with fresh basil leaves, if desired.
Slice and serve your delicious four cheese pizza! Enjoy the rich and creamy blend of cheeses.

Mushroom and Spinach Pizza
Ingredients:

- 1 pizza dough (store-bought or homemade)
- 1/2 cup pizza sauce

- 2 cups shredded mozzarella cheese
- 1 cup sliced mushrooms
- 2 cups fresh spinach leaves, washed and dried
- 2 cloves garlic, minced
- 2 tablespoons olive oil
- Salt and pepper to taste
- Crushed red pepper flakes (optional)
- Grated Parmesan cheese for garnish (optional)

Instructions:

Preheat your oven to 475°F (245°C). If using a pizza stone, place it in the oven to preheat as well.
Roll out the pizza dough on a floured surface to your desired thickness. Transfer it to a pizza peel or a lightly greased baking sheet.
In a skillet, heat 1 tablespoon of olive oil over medium heat. Add minced garlic and sauté until fragrant, about 1 minute.
Add sliced mushrooms to the skillet and cook until they are tender and browned, about 5-6 minutes. Season with salt and pepper to taste. Remove from heat and set aside.
Spread the pizza sauce evenly over the dough, leaving a small border around the edges.
Sprinkle the shredded mozzarella cheese over the sauce.
Evenly distribute the cooked mushrooms over the cheese.
Layer the fresh spinach leaves over the mushrooms.
Drizzle the remaining olive oil over the spinach and season with salt and pepper.
If desired, sprinkle with crushed red pepper flakes for some heat.
Carefully transfer the pizza to the preheated oven or pizza stone.
Bake for 10-12 minutes, or until the crust is golden brown and the cheese is bubbly and melted.
Remove the pizza from the oven and let it cool slightly.
Optionally, garnish with grated Parmesan cheese before serving.
Slice and enjoy your delicious mushroom and spinach pizza!

Spicy Sausage Pizza

Ingredients:

- 1 pizza dough (store-bought or homemade)
- 1/2 cup pizza sauce
- 2 cups shredded mozzarella cheese

- 1/2 lb spicy Italian sausage, casing removed and crumbled
- 1/4 cup sliced red onions
- 1/4 cup sliced green bell peppers
- 1/4 cup sliced jalapeños (optional, for extra heat)
- 2 cloves garlic, minced
- 1 tablespoon olive oil
- Crushed red pepper flakes (optional, for additional spice)
- Salt and pepper to taste

Instructions:

Preheat your oven to 475°F (245°C). If using a pizza stone, place it in the oven to preheat as well.

In a skillet, heat olive oil over medium heat. Add minced garlic and cook until fragrant, about 1 minute.

Add the crumbled spicy Italian sausage to the skillet. Cook until browned and cooked through, breaking it into smaller pieces with a spoon as it cooks, about 5-6 minutes. Drain excess fat if needed. Set aside.

Roll out the pizza dough on a floured surface to your desired thickness. Transfer it to a pizza peel or a lightly greased baking sheet.

Spread the pizza sauce evenly over the dough, leaving a small border around the edges.

Sprinkle the shredded mozzarella cheese over the sauce.

Evenly distribute the cooked spicy Italian sausage over the cheese.

Scatter the sliced red onions, green bell peppers, and jalapeños (if using) over the sausage.

Season with salt and pepper to taste. If desired, sprinkle with crushed red pepper flakes for extra heat.

Carefully transfer the pizza to the preheated oven or pizza stone.

Bake for 10-12 minutes, or until the crust is golden brown and the cheese is bubbly and melted.

Remove the pizza from the oven and let it cool slightly.

Slice and serve your delicious spicy sausage pizza! Enjoy the fiery flavors.

Pesto Chicken Pizza

Ingredients:

- 1 pizza dough (store-bought or homemade)
- 1/2 cup basil pesto (store-bought or homemade)

- 2 cups cooked chicken breast, shredded or diced
- 1 cup shredded mozzarella cheese
- 1/4 cup sliced sun-dried tomatoes (packed in oil, drained)
- 1/4 cup sliced black olives
- 2 cloves garlic, minced
- 2 tablespoons olive oil
- Salt and pepper to taste
- Fresh basil leaves for garnish (optional)

Instructions:

Preheat your oven to 475°F (245°C). If using a pizza stone, place it in the oven to preheat as well.

Roll out the pizza dough on a floured surface to your desired thickness. Transfer it to a pizza peel or a lightly greased baking sheet.

In a small bowl, mix together minced garlic and olive oil. Brush this mixture evenly over the surface of the pizza dough.

Spread the basil pesto evenly over the dough, leaving a small border around the edges.

Sprinkle the shredded mozzarella cheese over the pesto.

Evenly distribute the cooked chicken breast over the cheese.

Scatter the sliced sun-dried tomatoes and black olives over the chicken.

Season with salt and pepper to taste.

Carefully transfer the pizza to the preheated oven or pizza stone.

Bake for 10-12 minutes, or until the crust is golden brown and the cheese is bubbly and melted.

Remove the pizza from the oven and let it cool slightly.

Optionally, garnish with fresh basil leaves before serving.

Slice and enjoy your delicious pesto chicken pizza! The combination of flavors is sure to delight your taste buds.

Mediterranean Pizza

Ingredients:

- 1 pizza dough (store-bought or homemade)
- 1/2 cup pizza sauce or marinara sauce
- 1 cup shredded mozzarella cheese
- 1/2 cup crumbled feta cheese
- 1/4 cup sliced black olives

- 1/4 cup sliced sun-dried tomatoes (packed in oil, drained)
- 1/4 cup sliced roasted red peppers
- 1/4 cup thinly sliced red onions
- 2 cloves garlic, minced
- 2 tablespoons olive oil
- 1 teaspoon dried oregano
- Salt and pepper to taste
- Fresh basil leaves for garnish (optional)

Instructions:

Preheat your oven to 475°F (245°C). If using a pizza stone, place it in the oven to preheat as well.
Roll out the pizza dough on a floured surface to your desired thickness. Transfer it to a pizza peel or a lightly greased baking sheet.
In a small bowl, mix together minced garlic and olive oil. Brush this mixture evenly over the surface of the pizza dough.
Spread the pizza sauce evenly over the dough, leaving a small border around the edges.
Sprinkle the shredded mozzarella cheese over the sauce.
Evenly distribute the crumbled feta cheese, sliced black olives, sun-dried tomatoes, roasted red peppers, and thinly sliced red onions over the pizza.
Sprinkle dried oregano over the toppings.
Season with salt and pepper to taste.
Carefully transfer the pizza to the preheated oven or pizza stone.
Bake for 10-12 minutes, or until the crust is golden brown and the cheese is bubbly and melted.
Remove the pizza from the oven and let it cool slightly.
Optionally, garnish with fresh basil leaves before serving.
Slice and enjoy your delicious Mediterranean pizza! The combination of Mediterranean flavors will transport you to the sunny shores of the Mediterranean.

Smoked Salmon Pizza

Ingredients:

- 1 pizza dough (store-bought or homemade)
- 1/2 cup crème fraîche or sour cream
- 1 cup shredded mozzarella cheese

- 4 oz smoked salmon, thinly sliced
- 1/4 cup thinly sliced red onions
- 2 tablespoons capers, drained
- 2 tablespoons chopped fresh dill
- 1 lemon, cut into wedges
- Olive oil
- Salt and pepper to taste

Instructions:

Preheat your oven to 475°F (245°C). If using a pizza stone, place it in the oven to preheat as well.
Roll out the pizza dough on a floured surface to your desired thickness. Transfer it to a pizza peel or a lightly greased baking sheet.
Spread the crème fraîche or sour cream evenly over the dough, leaving a small border around the edges.
Sprinkle the shredded mozzarella cheese over the crème fraîche.
Arrange the thinly sliced smoked salmon over the cheese.
Scatter the thinly sliced red onions and capers over the salmon.
Drizzle a little olive oil over the top and season with salt and pepper to taste.
Carefully transfer the pizza to the preheated oven or pizza stone.
Bake for 10-12 minutes, or until the crust is golden brown and the cheese is bubbly and melted.
Remove the pizza from the oven and sprinkle chopped fresh dill over the top.
Serve hot with lemon wedges on the side for squeezing over the pizza.
Slice and enjoy your delicious smoked salmon pizza! The combination of flavors is sure to impress.

Roasted Garlic and Chicken Pizza

Ingredients:

- 1 pizza dough (store-bought or homemade)
- 1/2 cup pizza sauce or marinara sauce
- 2 cups shredded cooked chicken breast
- 1/2 cup roasted garlic cloves
- 1 cup shredded mozzarella cheese
- 1/4 cup grated Parmesan cheese
- 2 tablespoons olive oil
- Salt and pepper to taste

- Fresh parsley, chopped (for garnish)
- Crushed red pepper flakes (optional)

Instructions:

Preheat your oven to 475°F (245°C). If using a pizza stone, place it in the oven to preheat as well.
Roll out the pizza dough on a floured surface to your desired thickness. Transfer it to a pizza peel or a lightly greased baking sheet.
Brush olive oil over the surface of the pizza dough.
Spread the pizza sauce evenly over the dough, leaving a small border around the edges.
Evenly distribute the shredded cooked chicken breast over the sauce.
Scatter the roasted garlic cloves over the chicken.
Sprinkle the shredded mozzarella cheese and grated Parmesan cheese over the toppings.
Season with salt and pepper to taste. If desired, sprinkle with crushed red pepper flakes for extra heat.
Carefully transfer the pizza to the preheated oven or pizza stone.
Bake for 10-12 minutes, or until the crust is golden brown and the cheese is bubbly and melted.
Remove the pizza from the oven and let it cool slightly.
Garnish with chopped fresh parsley before serving.
Slice and enjoy your delicious roasted garlic and chicken pizza!

Sweetcorn and Bacon Pizza

Ingredients:

- 1 pizza dough (store-bought or homemade)
- 1/2 cup pizza sauce
- 1 cup shredded mozzarella cheese
- 1 cup sweetcorn kernels (fresh or canned, drained)
- 1/2 cup cooked bacon, chopped
- 1/4 cup sliced green onions (scallions)
- 1 tablespoon olive oil
- Salt and pepper to taste
- Red pepper flakes (optional)

Instructions:

Preheat your oven to 475°F (245°C). If using a pizza stone, place it in the oven to preheat as well.

Roll out the pizza dough on a floured surface to your desired thickness. Transfer it to a pizza peel or a lightly greased baking sheet.

Spread the pizza sauce evenly over the dough, leaving a small border around the edges.

Sprinkle the shredded mozzarella cheese over the sauce.

Evenly distribute the sweetcorn kernels and chopped cooked bacon over the cheese.

Scatter the sliced green onions over the toppings.

Drizzle olive oil over the top and season with salt and pepper to taste. If desired, sprinkle with red pepper flakes for extra heat.

Carefully transfer the pizza to the preheated oven or pizza stone.

Bake for 10-12 minutes, or until the crust is golden brown and the cheese is bubbly and melted.

Remove the pizza from the oven and let it cool slightly.

Slice and serve your delicious sweetcorn and bacon pizza! Enjoy the savory and sweet flavors.

Artichoke and Olive Pizza

Ingredients:

- 1 pizza dough (store-bought or homemade)
- 1/2 cup pizza sauce or marinara sauce
- 1 cup shredded mozzarella cheese
- 1 cup marinated artichoke hearts, drained and chopped
- 1/4 cup sliced black olives
- 2 tablespoons chopped fresh parsley
- 1 tablespoon olive oil
- 2 cloves garlic, minced
- Salt and pepper to taste
- Red pepper flakes (optional)

Instructions:

Preheat your oven to 475°F (245°C). If using a pizza stone, place it in the oven to preheat as well.

Roll out the pizza dough on a floured surface to your desired thickness. Transfer it to a pizza peel or a lightly greased baking sheet.

In a small bowl, mix together minced garlic and olive oil. Brush this mixture evenly over the surface of the pizza dough.

Spread the pizza sauce evenly over the dough, leaving a small border around the edges.

Sprinkle the shredded mozzarella cheese over the sauce.

Evenly distribute the chopped marinated artichoke hearts and sliced black olives over the cheese.

Season with salt and pepper to taste. If desired, sprinkle with red pepper flakes for some heat.

Carefully transfer the pizza to the preheated oven or pizza stone.

Bake for 10-12 minutes, or until the crust is golden brown and the cheese is bubbly and melted.

Remove the pizza from the oven and let it cool slightly.

Sprinkle chopped fresh parsley over the top before serving.

Slice and enjoy your delicious artichoke and olive pizza! The combination of flavors is sure to please.

Tandoori Chicken Pizza

Ingredients:

For Tandoori Chicken:

- 2 boneless, skinless chicken breasts
- 1/2 cup plain yogurt
- 2 tablespoons tandoori paste or powder
- 1 tablespoon lemon juice
- 2 cloves garlic, minced
- 1 teaspoon ginger paste (or minced ginger)
- 1/2 teaspoon ground cumin
- 1/2 teaspoon ground coriander
- 1/2 teaspoon paprika
- Salt and pepper to taste

For Pizza:

- 1 pizza dough (store-bought or homemade)
- 1/2 cup pizza sauce or marinara sauce
- 1 cup shredded mozzarella cheese
- 1/4 cup diced red onion
- 1/4 cup diced bell pepper (any color)
- 2 tablespoons chopped fresh cilantro (coriander)

- 1 tablespoon olive oil
- Salt and pepper to taste
- Lemon wedges (for serving)

Instructions:

Preheat your oven to 475°F (245°C). If using a pizza stone, place it in the oven to preheat as well.
In a bowl, mix together yogurt, tandoori paste or powder, lemon juice, minced garlic, ginger paste, ground cumin, ground coriander, paprika, salt, and pepper.
Add chicken breasts to the marinade, coating them well. Cover and refrigerate for at least 30 minutes, or preferably overnight.
Heat a grill or grill pan over medium-high heat. Grill the marinated chicken breasts until cooked through, about 6-8 minutes per side. Remove from the grill and let them cool slightly before dicing them into small pieces.
Roll out the pizza dough on a floured surface to your desired thickness. Transfer it to a pizza peel or a lightly greased baking sheet.
Spread the pizza sauce evenly over the dough, leaving a small border around the edges.
Sprinkle the shredded mozzarella cheese over the sauce.
Evenly distribute the diced tandoori chicken, diced red onion, and diced bell pepper over the cheese.
Drizzle olive oil over the toppings and season with salt and pepper to taste.
Carefully transfer the pizza to the preheated oven or pizza stone.
Bake for 10-12 minutes, or until the crust is golden brown and the cheese is bubbly and melted.
Remove the pizza from the oven and sprinkle chopped fresh cilantro over the top.
Serve hot with lemon wedges on the side for squeezing over the pizza.
Slice and enjoy your delicious tandoori chicken pizza!

Spinach and Feta Pizza

Ingredients:

- 1 pizza dough (store-bought or homemade)
- 1/2 cup pizza sauce or marinara sauce
- 2 cups fresh spinach leaves, washed and dried
- 1 cup crumbled feta cheese
- 1 cup shredded mozzarella cheese
- 1/4 cup sliced red onion
- 2 cloves garlic, minced

- 2 tablespoons olive oil
- Salt and pepper to taste
- Crushed red pepper flakes (optional)
- Grated Parmesan cheese for garnish (optional)

Instructions:

Preheat your oven to 475°F (245°C). If using a pizza stone, place it in the oven to preheat as well.

Roll out the pizza dough on a floured surface to your desired thickness. Transfer it to a pizza peel or a lightly greased baking sheet.

In a skillet, heat 1 tablespoon of olive oil over medium heat. Add minced garlic and sauté until fragrant, about 1 minute.

Add fresh spinach leaves to the skillet and cook until wilted, about 2-3 minutes. Season with salt and pepper to taste. Remove from heat and set aside.

Spread the pizza sauce evenly over the dough, leaving a small border around the edges.

Sprinkle the shredded mozzarella cheese over the sauce.

Evenly distribute the cooked spinach over the cheese.

Sprinkle the crumbled feta cheese and sliced red onion over the spinach.

Drizzle the remaining olive oil over the toppings.

If desired, sprinkle with crushed red pepper flakes for some heat.

Carefully transfer the pizza to the preheated oven or pizza stone.

Bake for 10-12 minutes, or until the crust is golden brown and the cheese is bubbly and melted.

Remove the pizza from the oven and let it cool slightly.

Optionally, garnish with grated Parmesan cheese before serving.

Slice and enjoy your delicious spinach and feta pizza! The combination of flavors is sure to please.

Caprese Pizza

Ingredients:

- 1 pizza dough (store-bought or homemade)
- 1/2 cup pizza sauce or marinara sauce
- 2 large tomatoes, thinly sliced
- 8 oz fresh mozzarella cheese, thinly sliced
- 1/4 cup fresh basil leaves
- 2 tablespoons balsamic glaze
- 2 cloves garlic, minced

- 2 tablespoons olive oil
- Salt and pepper to taste

Instructions:

Preheat your oven to 475°F (245°C). If using a pizza stone, place it in the oven to preheat as well.

Roll out the pizza dough on a floured surface to your desired thickness. Transfer it to a pizza peel or a lightly greased baking sheet.

In a small bowl, mix minced garlic with olive oil. Brush the garlic-infused olive oil evenly over the surface of the pizza dough.

Spread the pizza sauce evenly over the dough, leaving a small border around the edges.

Arrange the thinly sliced tomatoes over the sauce.

Place the fresh mozzarella slices evenly over the tomatoes.

Tear the fresh basil leaves and scatter them over the pizza.

Season with salt and pepper to taste.

Carefully transfer the pizza to the preheated oven or pizza stone.

Bake for 10-12 minutes, or until the crust is golden brown and the cheese is melted and bubbly.

Remove the pizza from the oven and drizzle the balsamic glaze over the top.

Let the pizza cool slightly before slicing.

Slice and serve your delicious Caprese pizza! Enjoy the fresh and vibrant flavors.

Meatball Pizza

Ingredients:

For Meatballs:

- 1 lb ground beef
- 1/2 cup breadcrumbs
- 1/4 cup grated Parmesan cheese
- 1 egg
- 2 cloves garlic, minced
- 1 teaspoon dried oregano
- 1 teaspoon dried basil
- Salt and pepper to taste
- Olive oil (for frying)

For Pizza:

- 1 pizza dough (store-bought or homemade)
- 1/2 cup pizza sauce or marinara sauce
- 1 cup shredded mozzarella cheese
- 1/4 cup grated Parmesan cheese
- 1/4 cup sliced black olives
- 1/4 cup sliced red onions
- Fresh basil leaves for garnish (optional)

Instructions:

Preheat your oven to 475°F (245°C). If using a pizza stone, place it in the oven to preheat as well.
In a large mixing bowl, combine ground beef, breadcrumbs, grated Parmesan cheese, egg, minced garlic, dried oregano, dried basil, salt, and pepper. Mix until well combined.
Roll the mixture into meatballs, about 1 inch in diameter.
Heat olive oil in a skillet over medium heat. Cook the meatballs until browned on all sides and cooked through, about 8-10 minutes. Remove from heat and set aside.
Roll out the pizza dough on a floured surface to your desired thickness. Transfer it to a pizza peel or a lightly greased baking sheet.
Spread the pizza sauce evenly over the dough, leaving a small border around the edges.
Sprinkle the shredded mozzarella cheese over the sauce.
Place the cooked meatballs evenly over the cheese.
Scatter sliced black olives and sliced red onions over the meatballs.
Sprinkle grated Parmesan cheese over the top.
Carefully transfer the pizza to the preheated oven or pizza stone.
Bake for 10-12 minutes, or until the crust is golden brown and the cheese is bubbly and melted.
Remove the pizza from the oven and let it cool slightly.
Garnish with fresh basil leaves before serving, if desired.
Slice and enjoy your delicious meatball pizza!

Buffalo Chicken Pizza
Ingredients:
For Buffalo Chicken:

- 2 boneless, skinless chicken breasts
- 1/2 cup buffalo sauce

- 2 tablespoons unsalted butter, melted
- 1 tablespoon olive oil
- Salt and pepper to taste

For Pizza:

- 1 pizza dough (store-bought or homemade)
- 1/4 cup buffalo sauce (for pizza)
- 1/2 cup ranch or blue cheese dressing
- 1 cup shredded mozzarella cheese
- 1/4 cup crumbled blue cheese (optional)
- 2 green onions, thinly sliced
- 1/4 cup diced red onion (optional)
- 1/4 cup chopped celery (optional)

Instructions:

Preheat your oven to 475°F (245°C). If using a pizza stone, place it in the oven to preheat as well.

Season chicken breasts with salt and pepper. Heat olive oil in a skillet over medium-high heat. Cook the chicken breasts until golden brown and cooked through, about 6-8 minutes per side. Remove from heat and let them cool slightly before shredding them into bite-sized pieces.

In a bowl, mix together shredded chicken, buffalo sauce, melted butter, and additional salt and pepper to taste.

Roll out the pizza dough on a floured surface to your desired thickness. Transfer it to a pizza peel or a lightly greased baking sheet.

Spread the buffalo sauce evenly over the dough, leaving a small border around the edges.

Drizzle ranch or blue cheese dressing over the buffalo sauce.

Sprinkle shredded mozzarella cheese over the sauce.

Evenly distribute the shredded buffalo chicken over the cheese.

If using, scatter crumbled blue cheese, sliced green onions, diced red onion, and chopped celery over the top.

Carefully transfer the pizza to the preheated oven or pizza stone.

Bake for 10-12 minutes, or until the crust is golden brown and the cheese is bubbly and melted.

Remove the pizza from the oven and let it cool slightly.

Slice and serve your delicious buffalo chicken pizza! Enjoy the spicy and savory flavors.

Prosciutto and Arugula Pizza

Ingredients:

- 1 pizza dough (store-bought or homemade)
- 1/2 cup pizza sauce or marinara sauce
- 1 cup shredded mozzarella cheese
- 4 oz prosciutto, thinly sliced
- 2 cups fresh arugula
- 1 tablespoon olive oil
- 1 tablespoon balsamic glaze
- Salt and pepper to taste

Instructions:

Preheat your oven to 475°F (245°C). If using a pizza stone, place it in the oven to preheat as well.

Roll out the pizza dough on a floured surface to your desired thickness. Transfer it to a pizza peel or a lightly greased baking sheet.

Spread the pizza sauce evenly over the dough, leaving a small border around the edges.

Sprinkle the shredded mozzarella cheese over the sauce.

Arrange the thinly sliced prosciutto over the cheese.

Carefully transfer the pizza to the preheated oven or pizza stone.

Bake for 10-12 minutes, or until the crust is golden brown and the cheese is bubbly and melted.

While the pizza is baking, in a small bowl, toss the arugula with olive oil, balsamic glaze, salt, and pepper to taste.

Remove the pizza from the oven and let it cool slightly.

Evenly distribute the dressed arugula over the top of the hot pizza.

Slice and serve your delicious prosciutto and arugula pizza! Enjoy the combination of flavors and textures.

Goat Cheese and Caramelized Onion Pizza

Ingredients:

- 1 pizza dough (store-bought or homemade)
- 2 tablespoons olive oil

- 2 large onions, thinly sliced
- 1 tablespoon balsamic vinegar
- Salt and pepper to taste
- 1 cup crumbled goat cheese
- 1 cup shredded mozzarella cheese
- 2 tablespoons chopped fresh thyme
- 1 tablespoon honey (optional)
- Red pepper flakes (optional)

Instructions:

Preheat your oven to 475°F (245°C). If using a pizza stone, place it in the oven to preheat as well.

Heat olive oil in a large skillet over medium heat. Add the thinly sliced onions and cook, stirring occasionally, until they are caramelized and golden brown, about 20-25 minutes.

Stir in balsamic vinegar and continue cooking for another 2-3 minutes until the vinegar has evaporated. Season with salt and pepper to taste. Set aside.

Roll out the pizza dough on a floured surface to your desired thickness. Transfer it to a pizza peel or a lightly greased baking sheet.

Spread the caramelized onions evenly over the dough, leaving a small border around the edges.

Sprinkle the crumbled goat cheese and shredded mozzarella cheese over the onions.

Sprinkle chopped fresh thyme over the cheese.

If desired, drizzle honey over the top for a touch of sweetness.

If you prefer some heat, sprinkle red pepper flakes over the pizza.

Carefully transfer the pizza to the preheated oven or pizza stone.

Bake for 10-12 minutes, or until the crust is golden brown and the cheese is bubbly and melted.

Remove the pizza from the oven and let it cool slightly.

Slice and serve your delicious goat cheese and caramelized onion pizza! Enjoy the rich and savory flavors.

Fig and Gorgonzola Pizza

Ingredients:

- 1 pizza dough (store-bought or homemade)
- 1/2 cup fig preserves
- 4 oz Gorgonzola cheese, crumbled

- 1/2 cup shredded mozzarella cheese
- 1/4 cup chopped walnuts
- Fresh thyme leaves for garnish (optional)
- Olive oil for drizzling

Instructions:

Preheat your oven to 475°F (245°C). If using a pizza stone, place it in the oven to preheat as well.

Roll out the pizza dough on a floured surface to your desired thickness. Transfer it to a pizza peel or a lightly greased baking sheet.

Spread the fig preserves evenly over the dough, leaving a small border around the edges.

Sprinkle the crumbled Gorgonzola cheese and shredded mozzarella cheese over the fig preserves.

Scatter the chopped walnuts over the cheese.

Drizzle a little olive oil over the top.

Carefully transfer the pizza to the preheated oven or pizza stone.

Bake for 10-12 minutes, or until the crust is golden brown and the cheese is bubbly and melted.

Remove the pizza from the oven and let it cool slightly.

Garnish with fresh thyme leaves, if desired.

Slice and serve your delicious fig and Gorgonzola pizza! Enjoy the unique and delightful combination of flavors.

Shrimp Scampi Pizza

Ingredients:

- 1 pizza dough (store-bought or homemade)
- 1/2 cup Alfredo sauce or garlic butter sauce
- 1 cup cooked shrimp, peeled and deveined
- 2 tablespoons unsalted butter
- 3 cloves garlic, minced
- 1 tablespoon lemon juice
- 1/4 cup chopped fresh parsley
- 1 cup shredded mozzarella cheese
- 1/4 cup grated Parmesan cheese
- Salt and pepper to taste
- Crushed red pepper flakes (optional)

Instructions:

Preheat your oven to 475°F (245°C). If using a pizza stone, place it in the oven to preheat as well.

In a skillet, melt the unsalted butter over medium heat. Add minced garlic and cook until fragrant, about 1 minute.

Add the cooked shrimp to the skillet and sauté for 2-3 minutes until heated through.

Stir in lemon juice and chopped fresh parsley. Season with salt and pepper to taste. Remove from heat and set aside.

Roll out the pizza dough on a floured surface to your desired thickness. Transfer it to a pizza peel or a lightly greased baking sheet.

Spread the Alfredo sauce or garlic butter sauce evenly over the dough, leaving a small border around the edges.

Sprinkle the shredded mozzarella cheese over the sauce.

Evenly distribute the cooked shrimp mixture over the cheese.

Sprinkle the grated Parmesan cheese over the top.

If desired, sprinkle with crushed red pepper flakes for some heat.

Carefully transfer the pizza to the preheated oven or pizza stone.

Bake for 10-12 minutes, or until the crust is golden brown and the cheese is bubbly and melted.

Remove the pizza from the oven and let it cool slightly.

Slice and serve your delicious shrimp scampi pizza! Enjoy the flavors of the classic dish on a pizza crust.

Chicken Alfredo Pizza

Ingredients:

- 1 pizza dough (store-bought or homemade)
- 1/2 cup Alfredo sauce
- 1 cup cooked chicken breast, shredded or diced
- 1 cup shredded mozzarella cheese
- 1/4 cup grated Parmesan cheese
- 2 cloves garlic, minced
- 1 tablespoon olive oil
- Salt and pepper to taste
- Fresh parsley, chopped (for garnish)

Instructions:

Preheat your oven to 475°F (245°C). If using a pizza stone, place it in the oven to preheat as well.

Roll out the pizza dough on a floured surface to your desired thickness. Transfer it to a pizza peel or a lightly greased baking sheet.

In a small bowl, mix together minced garlic and olive oil. Brush this mixture evenly over the surface of the pizza dough.

Spread the Alfredo sauce evenly over the dough, leaving a small border around the edges.

Sprinkle the shredded mozzarella cheese over the sauce.

Evenly distribute the cooked chicken breast over the cheese.

Sprinkle the grated Parmesan cheese over the top.

Season with salt and pepper to taste.

Carefully transfer the pizza to the preheated oven or pizza stone.

Bake for 10-12 minutes, or until the crust is golden brown and the cheese is bubbly and melted.

Remove the pizza from the oven and let it cool slightly.

Garnish with chopped fresh parsley before serving.

Slice and enjoy your delicious chicken Alfredo pizza!

Steak and Blue Cheese Pizza

Ingredients:

- 1 pizza dough (store-bought or homemade)
- 8 oz cooked steak, thinly sliced
- 1/2 cup blue cheese, crumbled
- 1 cup shredded mozzarella cheese
- 1/4 cup sliced red onion
- 2 tablespoons olive oil
- 2 cloves garlic, minced
- Salt and pepper to taste
- Fresh parsley, chopped (for garnish)

Instructions:

Preheat your oven to 475°F (245°C). If using a pizza stone, place it in the oven to preheat as well.

Roll out the pizza dough on a floured surface to your desired thickness. Transfer it to a pizza peel or a lightly greased baking sheet.

In a small bowl, mix together minced garlic and olive oil. Brush this mixture evenly over the surface of the pizza dough.

Spread the shredded mozzarella cheese evenly over the dough, leaving a small border around the edges.

Evenly distribute the cooked steak slices over the cheese.

Sprinkle the crumbled blue cheese and sliced red onion over the steak.

Season with salt and pepper to taste.

Carefully transfer the pizza to the preheated oven or pizza stone.

Bake for 10-12 minutes, or until the crust is golden brown and the cheese is bubbly and melted.

Remove the pizza from the oven and let it cool slightly.

Garnish with chopped fresh parsley before serving.

Slice and enjoy your delicious steak and blue cheese pizza!

Sundried Tomato and Pesto Pizza

Ingredients:

- 1 pizza dough (store-bought or homemade)
- 1/2 cup basil pesto
- 1/2 cup shredded mozzarella cheese
- 1/4 cup chopped sun-dried tomatoes (packed in oil, drained)
- 1/4 cup sliced black olives
- 2 cloves garlic, minced
- 2 tablespoons olive oil
- Salt and pepper to taste
- Fresh basil leaves for garnish (optional)

Instructions:

Preheat your oven to 475°F (245°C). If using a pizza stone, place it in the oven to preheat as well.

Roll out the pizza dough on a floured surface to your desired thickness. Transfer it to a pizza peel or a lightly greased baking sheet.

In a small bowl, mix together minced garlic and olive oil. Brush this mixture evenly over the surface of the pizza dough.

Spread the basil pesto evenly over the dough, leaving a small border around the edges.

Sprinkle the shredded mozzarella cheese over the pesto.

Evenly distribute the chopped sun-dried tomatoes and sliced black olives over the cheese.

Season with salt and pepper to taste.

Carefully transfer the pizza to the preheated oven or pizza stone.

Bake for 10-12 minutes, or until the crust is golden brown and the cheese is bubbly and melted.

Remove the pizza from the oven and let it cool slightly.

Optionally, garnish with fresh basil leaves before serving.

Slice and enjoy your delicious sun-dried tomato and pesto pizza! The combination of flavors is sure to delight your taste buds.

Roasted Vegetable Pizza

Ingredients:

- 1 pizza dough (store-bought or homemade)
- 1/2 cup pizza sauce or marinara sauce
- 1 cup shredded mozzarella cheese
- 1 cup assorted roasted vegetables (such as bell peppers, zucchini, eggplant, mushrooms, and onions)
- 2 cloves garlic, minced
- 2 tablespoons olive oil
- Salt and pepper to taste
- Fresh basil leaves for garnish (optional)

Instructions:

Preheat your oven to 475°F (245°C). If using a pizza stone, place it in the oven to preheat as well.

Toss the assorted vegetables with minced garlic, olive oil, salt, and pepper.

Spread them out on a baking sheet in a single layer and roast in the preheated oven for 15-20 minutes, or until tender and slightly caramelized.

Roll out the pizza dough on a floured surface to your desired thickness. Transfer it to a pizza peel or a lightly greased baking sheet.

Spread the pizza sauce evenly over the dough, leaving a small border around the edges.

Sprinkle the shredded mozzarella cheese over the sauce.

Evenly distribute the roasted vegetables over the cheese.

Season with additional salt and pepper to taste, if desired.

Carefully transfer the pizza to the preheated oven or pizza stone.

Bake for 10-12 minutes, or until the crust is golden brown and the cheese is bubbly and melted.

Remove the pizza from the oven and let it cool slightly.

Optionally, garnish with fresh basil leaves before serving.

Slice and enjoy your delicious roasted vegetable pizza! The combination of flavors and textures is sure to please.

White Clam Pizza

Ingredients:

- 1 pizza dough (store-bought or homemade)
- 1/2 cup Alfredo sauce or garlic butter sauce
- 1 cup shredded mozzarella cheese
- 2 cloves garlic, minced
- 1 tablespoon olive oil
- 1/2 teaspoon crushed red pepper flakes (optional)
- 1/4 cup grated Parmesan cheese
- 2 cans (6.5 oz each) chopped clams, drained
- 2 tablespoons chopped fresh parsley
- Salt and pepper to taste
- Lemon wedges for serving (optional)

Instructions:

Preheat your oven to 475°F (245°C). If using a pizza stone, place it in the oven to preheat as well.

In a small bowl, mix together minced garlic and olive oil. Brush this mixture evenly over the surface of the pizza dough.

Spread the Alfredo sauce or garlic butter sauce evenly over the dough, leaving a small border around the edges.

Sprinkle the shredded mozzarella cheese over the sauce.

Evenly distribute the drained chopped clams over the cheese.

Season with salt, pepper, and crushed red pepper flakes (if using).

Sprinkle the grated Parmesan cheese over the top.

Carefully transfer the pizza to the preheated oven or pizza stone.

Bake for 10-12 minutes, or until the crust is golden brown and the cheese is bubbly and melted.

Remove the pizza from the oven and let it cool slightly.

Sprinkle chopped fresh parsley over the top before serving.

Optionally, serve with lemon wedges on the side for squeezing over the pizza.

Slice and enjoy your delicious white clam pizza! The flavors are reminiscent of the classic dish.

Thai Chicken Pizza

Ingredients:

For Thai Peanut Sauce:

- 1/4 cup creamy peanut butter
- 2 tablespoons soy sauce
- 1 tablespoon rice vinegar
- 1 tablespoon honey
- 1 clove garlic, minced
- 1 teaspoon grated fresh ginger
- 1/2 teaspoon sesame oil
- 1/4 teaspoon crushed red pepper flakes (optional)
- 2-3 tablespoons water, to thin the sauce

For Pizza:

- 1 pizza dough (store-bought or homemade)
- 1 cup cooked chicken breast, shredded or diced
- 1/2 cup shredded mozzarella cheese
- 1/2 cup shredded carrots
- 1/4 cup thinly sliced red bell pepper
- 1/4 cup thinly sliced green onions
- 2 tablespoons chopped fresh cilantro (coriander)
- Crushed peanuts for garnish (optional)

Instructions:

Preheat your oven to 475°F (245°C). If using a pizza stone, place it in the oven to preheat as well.

In a small saucepan over low heat, combine all the ingredients for the Thai peanut sauce except for water. Stir until smooth and well combined.

Gradually add water, 1 tablespoon at a time, until the sauce reaches your desired consistency. Remove from heat and set aside.

Roll out the pizza dough on a floured surface to your desired thickness. Transfer it to a pizza peel or a lightly greased baking sheet.

Spread the Thai peanut sauce evenly over the dough, leaving a small border around the edges.

Sprinkle the shredded mozzarella cheese over the sauce.

Evenly distribute the cooked chicken breast, shredded carrots, sliced red bell pepper, and sliced green onions over the cheese.

Carefully transfer the pizza to the preheated oven or pizza stone.

Bake for 10-12 minutes, or until the crust is golden brown and the cheese is bubbly and melted.

Remove the pizza from the oven and let it cool slightly.

Garnish with chopped fresh cilantro and crushed peanuts (if using) before serving.

Slice and enjoy your delicious Thai chicken pizza! The combination of flavors is sure to tantalize your taste buds.

Brie and Cranberry Pizza

Ingredients:

- 1 pizza dough (store-bought or homemade)
- 1/2 cup cranberry sauce (homemade or store-bought)
- 6 oz Brie cheese, sliced
- 1/4 cup chopped walnuts
- Fresh thyme leaves for garnish (optional)
- Olive oil for drizzling

Instructions:

Preheat your oven to 475°F (245°C). If using a pizza stone, place it in the oven to preheat as well.

Roll out the pizza dough on a floured surface to your desired thickness. Transfer it to a pizza peel or a lightly greased baking sheet.

Spread the cranberry sauce evenly over the dough, leaving a small border around the edges.

Arrange the sliced Brie cheese over the cranberry sauce.

Sprinkle the chopped walnuts over the cheese.

Drizzle a little olive oil over the top.

Carefully transfer the pizza to the preheated oven or pizza stone.

Bake for 10-12 minutes, or until the crust is golden brown and the cheese is melted and bubbly.

Remove the pizza from the oven and let it cool slightly.

Optionally, garnish with fresh thyme leaves before serving.

Slice and enjoy your delicious Brie and cranberry pizza! The combination of sweet and savory flavors is sure to be a hit.

Pulled Pork Pizza

Ingredients:

- 1 pizza dough (store-bought or homemade)
- 1/2 cup BBQ sauce
- 1 cup cooked pulled pork
- 1 cup shredded mozzarella cheese
- 1/4 cup sliced red onion
- 1/4 cup chopped fresh cilantro (coriander)
- Olive oil for drizzling

Instructions:

Preheat your oven to 475°F (245°C). If using a pizza stone, place it in the oven to preheat as well.

Roll out the pizza dough on a floured surface to your desired thickness. Transfer it to a pizza peel or a lightly greased baking sheet.

Spread the BBQ sauce evenly over the dough, leaving a small border around the edges.

Evenly distribute the cooked pulled pork over the sauce.

Sprinkle the shredded mozzarella cheese over the pulled pork.

Scatter sliced red onion over the cheese.

Drizzle a little olive oil over the top.

Carefully transfer the pizza to the preheated oven or pizza stone.

Bake for 10-12 minutes, or until the crust is golden brown and the cheese is melted and bubbly.

Remove the pizza from the oven and let it cool slightly.

Sprinkle chopped fresh cilantro over the top before serving.

Slice and enjoy your delicious pulled pork pizza! The smoky flavors of the BBQ sauce and pork are sure to satisfy.

Barbecue Bacon Pizza

Ingredients:

- 1 pizza dough (store-bought or homemade)
- 1/2 cup BBQ sauce

- 1 cup cooked and crumbled bacon
- 1 cup shredded mozzarella cheese
- 1/4 cup thinly sliced red onion
- 1/4 cup chopped fresh cilantro (coriander)
- Olive oil for drizzling

Instructions:

Preheat your oven to 475°F (245°C). If using a pizza stone, place it in the oven to preheat as well.
Roll out the pizza dough on a floured surface to your desired thickness. Transfer it to a pizza peel or a lightly greased baking sheet.
Spread the BBQ sauce evenly over the dough, leaving a small border around the edges.
Evenly distribute the cooked and crumbled bacon over the sauce.
Sprinkle the shredded mozzarella cheese over the bacon.
Scatter thinly sliced red onion over the cheese.
Drizzle a little olive oil over the top.
Carefully transfer the pizza to the preheated oven or pizza stone.
Bake for 10-12 minutes, or until the crust is golden brown and the cheese is melted and bubbly.
Remove the pizza from the oven and let it cool slightly.
Sprinkle chopped fresh cilantro over the top before serving.
Slice and enjoy your delicious barbecue bacon pizza! The combination of smoky bacon and tangy BBQ sauce is irresistible.

Sausage and Ricotta Pizza

Ingredients:

- 1 pizza dough (store-bought or homemade)
- 1/2 cup pizza sauce or marinara sauce
- 1 cup cooked Italian sausage, crumbled
- 1 cup ricotta cheese
- 1 cup shredded mozzarella cheese
- 1/4 cup grated Parmesan cheese
- 2 cloves garlic, minced
- 2 tablespoons olive oil
- Salt and pepper to taste
- Fresh basil leaves for garnish (optional)

Instructions:

Preheat your oven to 475°F (245°C). If using a pizza stone, place it in the oven to preheat as well.
Roll out the pizza dough on a floured surface to your desired thickness. Transfer it to a pizza peel or a lightly greased baking sheet.
In a small bowl, mix together minced garlic and olive oil. Brush this mixture evenly over the surface of the pizza dough.
Spread the pizza sauce evenly over the dough, leaving a small border around the edges.
Evenly distribute the crumbled Italian sausage over the sauce.
Drop spoonfuls of ricotta cheese evenly over the sausage.
Sprinkle the shredded mozzarella cheese and grated Parmesan cheese over the top.
Season with salt and pepper to taste.
Carefully transfer the pizza to the preheated oven or pizza stone.
Bake for 10-12 minutes, or until the crust is golden brown and the cheese is bubbly and melted.
Remove the pizza from the oven and let it cool slightly.
Optionally, garnish with fresh basil leaves before serving.
Slice and enjoy your delicious sausage and ricotta pizza! The creamy ricotta complements the savory sausage perfectly.

Chicken Tikka Masala Pizza